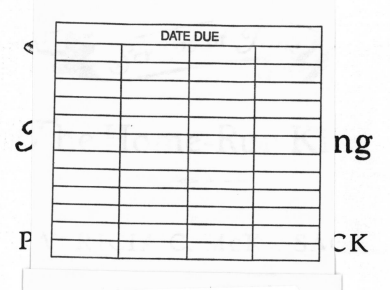

To Jaylan William Davis
Welcome to the family—P. C. McK.

To Ryan Johnson, a fine young man
and an awesome baseball player.—G. C. J.

ISBN: 978-0-545-23493-1

12 11 10 9 8 7 6 5 4 3   10 11 12 13 14 15/0

Printed in the U.S.A.   40

First Scholastic printing, January 2010

Set in Excelsior
Book design by Nancy Brennan

Contents

In Gee's Attic

There was always something new for the cousins to discover in their grandmother's attic. Well, "new" wasn't the right word. There was always something old to discover—things that had belonged to different people in their family, most of whom had lived long before Trey, Aggie, or Mattie Rae was born.

Earlier, Gee had told them about Aunt Lilly Belle Turner, who had gone to New York to study writing. Now Trey wanted to hear all about a baseball that had belonged to Lilly Belle's brothers.

"Everybody always called the Turner brothers by their nicknames, Tank and Jimbo," Gee

explained. "All except Lilly Belle. To her they were always Peter and James."

"Who gave them this ball?" Mattie Rae asked.

"Josh Gibson. He was the slugger on the Homestead Grays," Gee answered. "See his autograph? There are other ones, too."

Trey took the ball from Mattie Rae. "Satchel Paige signed this! He was a great pitcher," he said. "He's in the Baseball Hall of Fame."

"Tank and Jimbo knew players in the Hall of Fame?" Aggie was impressed.

"Tell us more about Tank and Jimbo," Trey asked.

Mattie Rae was still trying to get the base-ball back from Trey, until Gee handed her an old photo from the trunk.

Gee sat on a stool and began her story. "This is a picture of the Homestead Grays."

"You mean there were teams with just black players?" Mattie Rae said.

"Oh, yes. None of the major-league teams would let blacks play. And back in 1937 when this photo was taken, the Homestead Grays were as good as any major-league team around—or better."

Chapter 1

Caught!

James and Peter Turner looked like twins, even though James was a full year older than Peter. Now, with their sister Lilly Belle working at a Pittsburgh newspaper, there wasn't anybody in Nashville, Tennessee, who called the boys by their real names. James was Jimbo and Peter was Tank. They did everything together, and what they loved best was playing baseball. If only they had a team to play on . . . and other teams to play against.

They hardly ever got to watch games either.

But then Tank found a way to sneak into the Sulphur Springs Ballpark to see the Negro Leagues games. For free! It was risky, though.

Big, bad Joe Munday was the ballpark manager.

"I know you squirrels are sneakin' and peekin' but I'll catch you one of these days," Mr. Munday had told the brothers many times. "And when I do, I'm gonna call the police!"

"But we're just kids," said Tank, who was eleven.

"Old enough to go to the Tennessee State chain gang." Then Mr. Munday lowered his voice. "You'll be crackin' rocks from sunup till sundown for the rest of your lives."

Still Tank decided that watching a good baseball game was worth the risk. See, Tank loved taking chances. Like when Sammy Franklin double-dared Tank to ride down Deacon Hill freehanded on his bicycle. It was crazy, but Tank did it. Of course, he fell and broke his nose. But when Sammy called Tank a fool, it was Jimbo who tried to break Sammy's nose.

Tank always counted on his brother to have his back. So he went on his merry way, getting into hot water and expecting Jimbo to fish him out. And that's why Jimbo followed Tank whenever he sneaked into the ballpark.

It was a hot day in June. The Homestead Grays were playing the Tennessee All-Stars in a five game series, over the next eight days.

Same as always, Tank pushed aside the loose board in the fence behind the center-field bleachers. The opening was just large enough for him and Jimbo to squeeze through. Then they crawled on their bellies under the bleachers until they found a perfect spot to watch the game.

The boys were especially excited today, because

the Grays had one of the greatest new players. Josh Gibson had just joined the team. Tank already knew about him. He read everything he could on the Negro League players. Josh was a home-run threat every time he came to bat. Ordinarily Tank and Jimbo rooted for the Tennessee team, but the Grays were special. With Josh Gibson, they could make the 1937 season one of the best ever in the National Negro Baseball League!

The umpire yelled, "Batter up!"

Tank watched Josh Gibson take long strides to home plate. He was a muscular man with powerful arms and a big smile. He set his bat. The All-Star pitcher, Lee Webb, hurled two balls and then a blazing fastball strike.

"Look at him," Tank shouted. "Gibson is holding the bat with one hand now."

"Yeah, just like Babe Ruth!" said Jimbo. "He's mocking the pitcher."

Gibson pointed to right field.

"Look! He's showing where he's going to hit a homer!" said Jimbo.

"Do you think Gibson is as good as the Babe?" Tank asked.

"I think so," Jimbo said. "But there's no way to tell, 'cause coloreds can't play in the majors."

"One day they will," said Tank

"When pigs fly, maybe," Jimbo put in.

The pitcher was in the windup when suddenly, Tank felt two strong hands grab his feet and pull him backward.

"Run, Jimbo," shouted Tank. "Munday's got me!"

Jimbo crawled away on all fours and managed to escape.

"Ha! Finally got one of you squirrels," Mr. Munday said, and laughed. It sounded wicked.

Tank spit out dirt and coughed. Mr. Munday

dragged him to his feet. "Please, sir, don't put me on the chain gang. It would break my mother's heart," he pleaded.

All at once the crowd sent up a roar. Cheers and shouts hung on the muggy June air. Josh Gibson had hit a home run with one hand!

Munday cupped one hand over his eyes to follow the ball. "Look at it fly," he said, and then whistled through his teeth. For a brief moment he loosened his grip on Tank.

Tank twisted out of Munday's hold and dashed away.

"If I ever see you around this park again, you're gonna get it! Hear me?" Munday called after him, and shook his fist.

Tank never answered—never looked back or stopped running.

Chapter 2

Paying the Price

Tank caught up with Jimbo a block away from the stadium, and they jogged in a slow trot down Jefferson Street. Every once in a while, they looked back to make sure Munday wasn't following.

"That was a close call," said Jimbo.

"Too close for me," Tank replied.

They turned at 17th Street, down Johanna Street, then bounded up the steps of number 909. After a year, the boys were beginning to feel like the house was home, not a borrowed place.

"I got tired of rock farming," Daddy'd say, laughing. So he had sold his share of the Turner farmland to a company that quarried rock. Tank missed running in the wide-open fields. No cars to watch out for; no concrete to scrape his knees on.

Their new house was exactly like all the others on the street: a small, white-frame bungalow with a well-kept yard. The houses were built in the early 1900s by a man named August Diamond. So people began calling the area Diamond Row. People still did, but only a few remembered why.

Like a lot of women, Mama worked now. She ironed shirt cuffs and collars at the Rite Brite Laundry for a penny a shirt. Daddy was lucky enough to find work with the L&N Railroad as an oiler.

Times were hard in 1937. There was a Depression going on—too many people with not enough money or jobs.

Now that Lilly Belle had left home, the Turners had an extra bedroom. And like many other families on Diamond Row, they had a "room to rent" sign in their front window—one that Jimbo and Tank had made.

Today the sign was gone.

"Wonder who rented the room?" Tank said.

"We'll find out when Mama and Daddy get home," Jimbo said.

Less than an hour later, Jimbo and Tank were upstairs when the doorbell rang. They started downstairs and watched as Daddy answered the door.

It was Mr. Munday!

And with him was none other than Josh Gibson. Tank looked at his brother. He didn't know whether to shout for joy or scream in fear. They both crouched down to stay hidden.

They could hear Mr. Munday introduce himself and Josh Gibson to Daddy. All three men shook hands.

"Mighty nice what you've agreed to do, Mr. Turner," Mr. Munday said. "If it wasn't for the 'chitlin' circuit' our players would have nowhere to go."

Tank understood what Mr. Munday was talking about. The chitlin' circuit was the name for the group of sports arenas and theaters in different cities where blacks could play. Since colored people couldn't get rooms in white hotels or eat in white-owned restaurants, black families opened their homes to ballplayers, musicians, and other travelers.

"You have a lovely home," said Josh Gibson. "And I'll abide by all your rules . . . no whiskey and no smoking."

Daddy nodded his approval. "Those are my

wife's rules," he added with a smile. "I have to abide by them, too."

They all laughed. Daddy went on. "But I promise you'll be more comfortable than sleeping in the backseat of a car or in a bus."

"Some nights I've slept in fields," Josh replied. "Sleeping in a real bed these next few days will be pure luxury."

Jimbo and Tank stared at each other. Josh Gibson was staying in *their* house.

"Jimbo! Tank!" Daddy shouted. "Get down here and help take these bags up."

How lucky could an unlucky guy get? Tank muttered to himself. *Josh Gibson is staying in my house. And I'm going to be on a chain gang!*

Daddy called again.

Slowly Tank came down the steps. Jimbo followed. Mr. Munday's eyes widened. "You!" he shouted. "My runaway squirrels!"

Chapter 3

Gotcha!

After Daddy heard the story, he just shook his head.

"I caught this one red-handed today." Munday pointed to Tank. "But his brother got away."

Daddy blinked in disappointment. "Sons! You know we don't hold with stealing and cheating!"

"I didn't steal. . . ." Tank tried to argue.

"When you sneak into a ballpark while others have paid, that sure is stealing," Daddy said sharply. "Same as if you took money out of Mr. Munday's pocket."

"Daddy, don't let Mr. Munday send me to the chain gang!" Tank pleaded. "I can't bust rocks from sunup till sundown."

Jimbo spoke up. "I should have stopped Tank, Daddy. Instead, I went along with him."

Daddy gave Mr. Munday a questioning look. So did Josh Gibson.

"Did you tell these boys they were going to the chain gang?" Gibson asked.

Mr. Munday raised a finger. "Yes, I did. A day on the chain gang is fair punishment. Tank and Jimbo can work off their debt," he said, "if you'll agree, Mr. Turner."

Then Mr. Munday explained that the clean-up crew at the ballpark was called the chain gang. "They clean up after all home games. A day's work will pay off the price of a ticket."

"Sounds fair to me," said Daddy.

"Fine with me!" shouted Tank. He wouldn't

have to sneak in to see the game. He'd be right there! "Gee, thanks, Mr. Munday!"

Mr. Munday chuckled. "Tomorrow, report to my office. I'll introduce you to your crew chief. Four P.M. sharp. Don't be late."

"But the game starts at noon," Jimbo and Tank said at the same time.

"Yes. It should be over by four. Plenty of time to clean up before it gets dark."

"But I thought . . ." Tank said.

Mr. Munday chuckled again. "You thought you were going to get to see the game?"

Daddy and Josh Gibson looked as if they were about to burst out laughing.

"Gotcha!" And Mr. Munday bent over laughing.

"I knew it was too good to be true," Tank muttered as he pulled Josh Gibson's bag up the stairs.

Chapter 4

The Game Is Baseball

Before dinner, Tank and Jimbo headed for the backyard. Playing baseball was the one good thing about moving to the city. Tank read all about the teams in each of the two Negro Leagues. He knew the stats of all the great players.

Last spring Tank had learned how to hold a bat in school. And Jimbo was learning to pitch. Daddy had cut a piece of wood that almost looked like a real bat. He'd also filled a hollow rubber ball with sand. On the back porch he'd strung up a fishnet behind a rock that was home plate. The net was to catch the pitched balls. It wasn't a perfect setup, but Tank and Jimbo were happy.

Tank swung the makeshift bat several times. He tried it one-handed, like he'd seen Josh Gibson do. "Sometimes I wonder why we practice all the time. We don't have a team," Tank said.

"One day we might," said Jimbo. "Look, who woulda thought Josh Gibson would be sleeping in our house? And that happened."

Tank scoffed. "What good is it? We're not going to get to see him play!"

"We still got bragging rights!" Jimbo said. He picked up their baseball. Tank finally laughed, too.

"We'll get a ball club one day, and we'll be ready," Jimbo said.

Tank took his stance beside home base. Then he set his bat and waited for Jimbo's pitch.

"You're holding the bat too close to your body," Josh yelled from the upstairs window. "Loosen up some."

Tank looked up and grinned. "Like this?" he asked, bending his arms out.

"Better," said Gibson. "Now, stay focused. Put everything out of your mind except the bat and the ball."

"I'm going to hit a homer just like you, Mr. Gibson."

"Don't think about hitting a home run. Just hit the ball."

Jimbo released the pitch. It came at Tank fast and straight. Tank swung and hit a high fly ball. Jimbo easily caught it.

"Keep swinging like that and you'll be the world's best golfer," said Gibson. He clicked his teeth and shook his head. "If you swing down and up, you'll always hit fly balls. Next time, keep your bat level. Swing out from your shoulders."

Jimbo's next ball zoomed past Tank so fast he didn't see it.

"Great pitch, Jimbo," Josh called. "You've got speed. Now work on your control. Get it over the plate."

"Gosh, thanks, Mr. Gibson," Jimbo called up to him.

"Y'all call me Josh. Everybody does."

Tank knew that Jimbo's next pitch would be almost perfect. Tank could practice all day long and not be as good as Jimbo. Jimbo was a natural. . . . He never even seemed to be trying hard.

"Stuff comes easy for you," Tank said. "It's not fair. Remember when we were learning to ride a bike?"

Jimbo shrugged. "Your trouble is wanting to

be perfect. I just like to play and have fun."

Tank shook his head. What Jimbo said to him didn't make sense. Why do anything if you didn't plan to be the best?

Jimbo got ready to pitch again.

Then *pow*!

Tank slammed the ball. It soared deep into the backyard.

"Wow!" Tank yelled in triumph.

"Hey! That was good!" Josh exclaimed.

Tank cartwheeled halfway down the yard.

"Keep practicing, and you two will be a double threat on any team," said Josh. Then he closed the window and disappeared behind Mama's lace curtain.

Chapter 5

Foul

Mr. Munday was waiting for Tank and Jimbo at four o'clock sharp. The game was over. The Grays had won. Now the Sulphur Springs Ballpark was almost empty.

"That was the best game I've ever seen," Tank heard one fan saying. "Gibson is as good as they say and more. . . ."

"Looks like we missed a good one," Tank said. They saw Josh signing autographs. He waved to them. But the brothers had no time to say hello. Mr. Munday was shouting at them.

Next to Mr. Munday was a very tall guy with huge hands and huge feet.

"These two are on your chain gang," said Mr. Munday, introducing Tank and Jimbo to Apollo Monroe.

Apollo giggled. He covered his mouth to hide his teeth. Tank wondered how old Apollo was, but it was hard to tell. Older than either Tank or Jimbo, that was for sure. Apollo giggled again. That's when Tank realized that Apollo was an oversized boy. A forever kid.

"Hey," said Apollo in a big booming voice. All of him was just a little too much for the average person.

"Apollo," Tank said, smiling. "If I get in a fight, I want you on my team. Okay?"

"*Ooowee,*" said Apollo, jumping up and down, "I be on your team." Then he calmed down. "But you gotta do what I say or Uncle Munday will be mad at us," Apollo said softly. "Get your sack. Put it on. Follow me. One. Two. Three."

Mr. Munday was Apollo's uncle! Poor guy, Tank thought as they tied on big burlap sacks.

Apollo handed them each a broomstick with a nail driven into the end—that was how they picked up the trash.

Apollo said, "Now we line up like a big choo-choo. We go to Section C. Wheee!"

Everything was a game to Apollo, even cleanup.

When they were done with the bleachers, the boys brought the full trash bags back to Mr. Munday. Another crew was waiting to empty the bags into a large container behind the ballpark. In a few hours they'd finished.

"All done," Apollo said. He clapped his hands and waved.

"That it?" Jimbo asked when the three of them

dropped off their equipment at Mr. Munday's office.

"You want more to do?" Mr. Munday answered gruffly.

"It was so simple and easy, even an idiot could do it," Tank said without thinking.

"Even an idiot could do it," Apollo repeated slowly.

Jimbo's eyes turned toward Tank. Mr. Munday's, too. Tank wanted to cover his face. He felt hot all over. "No, no," Tank stumbled over his words. "I didn't mean that like it sounded. . . . I wouldn't . . . I was just talking. . . ."

"Go home," Mr. Munday said flatly. "Debt paid."

Tank wanted to explain. He liked Apollo! But just then Josh Gibson came through the office door.

"Don't tell me that you two are in trouble again," Josh said to the brothers.

"We paid off our debt for sneaking into the game," said Jimbo.

Yes, but they still had no way of seeing any games, Tank thought glumly. Then as if snatching an idea out of thin air, Tank spoke up. "Mr. Gibson. It's hot down here in Tennessee. Real hot."

"Tell me about it," he replied.

Tank hurried on. "What if my brother and I volunteer to be water boys for the Grays while you are in town. The All-Stars have local boys who work for them."

Josh rubbed his chin. "Ummm! Volunteer. Does that mean no pay?"

"Yes, sir."

"Sounds a'right to me. I'll speak to our manager about it. Give you an answer later on tonight. Your mama said she was serving up chicken and gravy for dinner. Look out! Here I come."

Chapter 6

A New Deal

On the way home, Jimbo was very quiet.

"What? What did I do now?" Tank asked with a shrug.

"What makes you think you can hire me out . . . and for no pay?"

"Look, the Grays will be back three or four more times," Tank explained. "Working as water boys, we get to see all their games for free. So in a way we are getting paid."

"You could have asked me first."

Tank headed up the porch steps. The smell of Mama's chicken filled the air. "There was no time. The idea came and I had to move on it."

During dinner Josh announced, "Our manager said you two could start at tomorrow's practice."

"What's this about?" Mama asked.

"Mama, Daddy, we're the Grays' new water boys," Tank explained. "Aren't we, Jimbo?"

"I guess," Jimbo said, agreeing. Tank flashed a big smile.

"Long as it doesn't interfere with your chores around here," said Daddy.

The boys quickly agreed.

"You have to be ready at dawn," Josh said. "Before it gets hot!"

After supper the boys helped Mama with the dishes, emptied the trash, and swept the kitchen floor.

Josh was sitting on the top porch step. Mama had put him to work churning a bucket of ice cream.

"Do you know Satchel Paige?" Jimbo asked him. "He's my favorite. No offense to you, Josh."

"That's a'right," he responded. Tank noticed how long Josh's fingers were. No wonder he could hold a bat with one hand and still smack the ball out of the ballpark.

"I know Satchel real good," Josh continued. "Sometimes we're teammates. Sometimes we're opponents."

"Is he as good a pitcher as they say?" Tank wanted to know.

"Better," Josh answered quickly. Then he leaned back. "He has names for his pitches— did you know that? Like the bee-ball. He says all a batter hears is the humming of the ball as it sings over the plate!"

"What about Cool Papa Bell?" Jimbo asked. "Is he really so fast?"

"You bet!" Josh answered. "They say when Cool Papa is ready to sleep, he can pull the light switch, then run hop into bed and pull up the covers before the light goes out."

They all laughed over that one.

"Now that's fast," said Josh.

"I want to be just like you when I grow up," Tank said.

Josh grinned. "You might want to pick a better person," he said.

"You're the Home-Run King," said Tank. "You can hit a homer one-handed."

Josh laughed. "I also strike out a lot, because I swing a lot," he added.

Mama brought out fresh-baked pound cake to go with the peach ice cream. She served everyone a big heaping bowl.

"My mama is the best cook in Davidson County," said Tank.

"I'm inclined to agree," said Josh as he began a story about the time he was playing off-season ball in Mexico City, Mexico, with Satchel Paige.

"They had me in center field and Satchel in right field. I forget who was on the left. Anyway, a batter hit a fast-moving grounder to right field. Satch easily scooped up the ball . . . and a snake as well. A year later, I ran into him in New York when we were playing the Cuban X-Giants. He said after seeing that snake, he didn't stop running—even over water—until he got back to the States!"

"Did that really happen?" Jimbo asked.

Josh grinned and winked an eye. "Well, some of it did," he answered.

"Doesn't matter," said Tank. "It's a funny, funny story."

Tank thought that evening was a little piece of heaven fallen to Johanna Street. It just couldn't get any better.

Chapter 7

Raw Deal

Tank and Jimbo managed to be at practice the next morning just as the sun was rising.

Tank studied Josh Gibson's every move. From the way he held his bat and the way he bit off a piece of chewing tobacco to the way he pivoted his foot and leveled his shoulder when he was getting ready to swing at a fastball, Josh did the same thing, the same way, all the time.

"I'm superstitious," he explained.

"It's super silly," Buck Leonard teased him.

Buck Leonard was a power-hitting first base-man for the Grays, and one of Tank's favorite players.

The most exciting thing for Tank was getting to hold a real bat. For Jimbo it was trying on Buck Leonard's glove.

That morning, the temperature had reached the upper nineties by eight thirty. Tank and Jim-bo scurried from one player to the next, bring-ing them water. They soaked towels in a bucket to wrap around the players' necks.

"Thanks, guys," the players said with pats on the back for Tank and Jimbo.

Tank loved being a water boy. He knew he was considered part of the team when one morn-ing right before practice, he put on his hat. There was a frog underneath.

Crrrrk! went the frog, and Tank's hat flew off his head.

"Who did this?" Tank asked. Then he noticed Josh and Buck Leonard were laughing just a little bit too hard.

The next day Jimbo saw to it that a frog ended up in Josh's pants pocket. Then it was Tank's turn to laugh.

"You brothers stick together," said Buck Leonard with a wink and a nod. "Teamwork! I like that!"

"Is teamwork more important than skill?" Jimbo asked.

"We play together as a team, and that improves our skills."

"Your team's got the best stats in the leagues," Tank said, "both the Negro National League and American Negro League. And you've got the best sluggers of any lineup. Josh can hit a home run with one hand! That's what I want to do. I want to hit one-handed homers one day!"

"Tank, look. It's not just home runs that win games. If we didn't work as a group, all we'd be is nine talented individuals. When we work together—presto—we're the Homestead Grays," Buck explained.

Tank was respectful, even though he didn't agree.

When the third game of the series ended with a Grays victory, the players rewarded Tank and Jimbo. They tipped them pennies and nickels, and somebody threw in a dime.

Tank and Jimbo headed straight for the corner store.

They met up with Apollo there. He was trying to decide what to buy.

"Candy . . . bad for teeth. Orange. That's it. No. I like apples better. Apples grow on trees. No need to buy one." Apollo took the apple and started to walk out.

"Look, that big dumb guy is stealing an apple," a boy yelled.

Apollo saw a clerk coming toward him who was yelling, "Stop! Thief!"

Apollo looked terrified. Tank tried to help. He tried to grab Apollo while he told the clerk, "He didn't mean any harm, mister."

But Apollo yanked away and lost his balance. A display of canned goods toppled over. The noise made Apollo cover his ears. He was so frightened he squatted in a corner and wailed pitifully.

"Don't be scared," Tank whispered to him. Then he turned to his brother. "Go get Mr. Munday, Jimbo."

Chapter 8

Done Deal

Mr. Munday arrived, paid for the apple, and took Apollo back to his office.

"Tank. He save me," said Apollo, sniffing as they began walking away. "But the man, he say I can't come in his store never no more."

Mr. Munday affectionately ruffled Apollo's hair. "I'm sorry. I know how you like going there yourself."

"Wait. Maybe we can help," said Tank.

Jimbo shook his head. "Hold on. . . ." But Tank

grabbed his brother by the arm and followed Mr. Munday and Apollo back toward the field.

"Tank is my friend," said Apollo. "He helps."

"What if we take Apollo to the store with us when we go? Huh?"

Jimbo had that *I don't believe you are volunteering us again* look on his face.

"We'll work with Apollo on the chain gang. Then we'll take him to the store."

"Ooweee!" said Apollo.

"You'd do that for me? For Apollo?" Mr. Munday said.

"Well"—Jimbo stepped in now—"not for free. We want to be paid for working on the chain gang." Then he looked at Tank and added, "Having fun with Apollo, we do for free."

Mr. Munday covered his face with his hands and sighed deeply. "Okay, how about you two clean up after each home game for twenty-five cents a month?"

"Twenty-five cents a month—each?" Jimbo said.

Mr. Munday thought that over as they arrived at the ball field. When they reached his office, Mr. Munday sat in his swivel chair and turned to face the window. With his back to the boys, he said, "Okay. Twenty cents a month each, and that's it."

"Done deal," said Tank.

Chapter 9

Red Rooster Chew

The Tennessee All-Stars put up a good fight against the Grays. After the fourth game, the teams were tied, two all. The last game in the series was set for Saturday at three P.M.

After lunch, the boys arrived at the stadium. Tank and Jimbo heard Josh before they saw him. All of his humor and good nature had gone sour.

"I can't hit without my chew," he was saying to the manager.

"Try mine," the manager offered.

Josh shoved it away. "No!"

"Tobacco is tobacco," said one of the players.

"No," said Tank. "Red Rooster is his brand. Nothing else will do."

"It settles my stomach and stills my nerves," said Josh. "Without my wad, I can't hit the broad side of a barn door. Aine been able to find any here except at the train station."

"That's ten blocks away," Jimbo whispered to Tank, and slipped him some money. "Think you can make it and get back in time?"

Tank smiled. "You bet!" Then he took off.

By the time Tank bought the tobacco and returned to the ballpark, the Grays were out in the field. Josh was taking his position behind the plate. Tank rushed over to Josh with the bag. "Hey! Thanks!" Josh said.

"That boy's got some extra legs somewhere," said one of the players.

"We got another Cool Papa Bell in the making," said Buck Leonard.

"Play ball," called the umpire.

Winded and tired, Tank caught his breath. Josh Gibson had his chewing tobacco. He went on to hit two home runs in one inning. And the Grays won the game 7–2, and the mini-series three out of five.

Later that night, while lying in bed, Tank told Jimbo, "Josh has a .425 batting average and it's just now June."

"Is that right? Really?" Josh called from the other room.

"Yes, Josh, you do," Daddy yelled from the downstairs bedroom. "Now go to sleep up there."

Chapter 10

Error Punishes Itself

With the series over, the Grays pulled out of town early the next morning. The house on Johanna Street was not the same without Josh. He had a way of filling up a space with his personality.

"Everything seems smaller and quieter without Josh," Tank said, sighing.

Jimbo missed seeing the games, but they still went to the ballpark to work on the chain gang and to watch out for Apollo.

On the way home from the stadium one day,

Tank said to Apollo and Jimbo, "Let's go to the store at the train station."

"Whatcha going to buy there?" Jimbo asked.

"You'll see," was all Tank said.

"I think Tank wants a ginger cookie," Apollo said once they reached the store. "I think I want a peppermint stick. No, Tank wants a peppermint stick."

Apollo saw Tank pick up a package with a rooster on the front. He shook his head. "No. No, Tank. No."

Apollo backed away. "No good." He rubbed his stomach and his head. "No good!"

"Apollo is right," said Jimbo. "He's got more sense than you!"

Tank handed over his money.

Outside the store, Tank opened the bag.

"This is what Josh Gibson chews, and he said he needs it to be the best." Tank took a big bite out of the tobacco. He chewed. He gave the twist to Jimbo, who pushed it away.

"Bad, bad bad bad bad!" Apollo said.

Tank didn't speak. He just shook his head, all the while chewing. His lips turned dark brown. He spat some juice out of his mouth like he had seen Josh do.

Slowly, Tank's face grew hot. Beads of sweat formed on his forehead and nose. The inside of his jaws burned like he'd eaten a hot pepper. He spat again. Then he chewed on the tobacco some more. He had to cough. When he did, some of the juice washed down his throat. That choked him, which made him swallow more of the juice.

"See! What'd I tell you!" Jimbo shouted.

Tank tried to walk but couldn't. He leaned against the side of a building. He was dizzy. His

stomach was flip-flopping like the day he ate too many unripe apples.

Tank spat out more tobacco juice and tobacco leaves.

"Yuck," said Apollo, hopping from foot to foot. "I go get help," he said. A few minutes later Apollo returned with Mr. Munday.

By then Tank was on his knees, moaning.

"Is he dying?" Apollo asked. His face was filled with worry.

"No, no, no," said Mr. Munday, chuckling, "but he's going to wish he was dead."

Brown juice oozed out of Tank's mouth. Then he heaved. It felt like his insides were coming out. The nasty taste in his mouth made him sicker. He heaved again.

"Tank, don't die," Apollo pleaded.

Mr. Munday was shaking his head. "All I can say is *error punishes itself*. I suspect you'll remember this bit of mischief for the rest of your life."

"That was not a smart thing to do," said Apollo.

"Apollo, sometimes you are a lot smarter than me," Tank said, just before he threw up again.

Chapter 11

A Team of Our Own

Tank's stomach was queasy for two days. "No more tobacco for me," he said.

Even though the Grays' games were over, the brothers still went to the ballpark for cleanup and to hang out with Apollo. Mr. Munday didn't seem to mind. In fact he wasn't so gruff anymore.

One day Tank, Jimbo, and Apollo were sitting in the bleachers talking.

"Wouldn't it be great to hit a home run in a stadium like this?" Tank said. "To wear a uniform?"

Jimbo shrugged. "I guess. I just want to play on a real team with a real coach. It wouldn't have to be in a stadium."

"Play here," said Apollo. "Play ball here."

Tank hopped up to a higher bleacher. "What did you say, Apollo?"

"I say, what I say," he answered, not the slightest bit confused.

Tank thought for a moment and grew excited.

"You said, 'Play ball here.' Thanks, Apollo! You gave me an idea."

"I want it back," said Apollo. "I didn't mean to give it away."

"I'm going to give it to your uncle," Tank explained. "Come with me."

Happily, Apollo followed Tank. Jimbo lagged behind. "What now, little brother?" he asked. "No surprises and no volunteering."

"Sir, Apollo gave me an idea," Tank said once

they were inside Mr. Munday's office. "What if you start a baseball team for colored boys here at the ballpark? We could practice and play in the stadium when no pro games are scheduled."

"Apollo gave you this idea?"

"Well, maybe not all of it," Tank replied.

Mr. Munday tried not to smile, but his eyes did. "A team costs money," he said.

"An empty stadium earns nothing," Tank argued.

"Everybody's daddy will come see us play; our mothers, aunts, and uncles will, too," Jimbo added.

Tank knew then that Jimbo liked his idea.

"The trouble is, we don't know enough people to make up a team. We're still the new kids," Jimbo said.

But Tank picked up from there. "I think kids

would play if there was a team to join. We could play other teams in the area."

"I'm not so sure about—" Mr. Munday said.

"We just want a chance to play baseball. Say you'll think about it, *please*?" Tank added, stretching the last word.

"Please!" chimed in Apollo.

"You three are quite convincing," said Mr. Munday. "Who would coach this team of yours?"

"You," said Jimbo. Tank shut up and let Jimbo move on. "Mr. Munday, I think you'd be a great coach."

Mr. Munday stood up and straightened his tie. "Do you really think so? I always sort of dreamed of . . . long ago . . . Well."

"And I play with you. Whee. I play today," Apollo said, picking up on the excitement.

Mr. Munday closed his eyes. "No, Apollo, I'm

very sorry. But you can't play on the team."

"But, Apollo, you can join us," Tank insisted. "You can be our water boy. How would you like that, Apollo? You can be our official water boy."

"Ooowee!"

Mr. Munday threw up his arms. "Hey, hold on here. You're giving out jobs for a nonexistent ball club. Let's see," he said, sitting back down in his swivel chair. "How does the name Red Roosters sound for a team?"

"We're a team!" shouted Tank.

Tank and Jimbo made posters announcing tryouts for the team. Then they stuffed flyers in mailboxes all over Diamond Row and North Nashville. Mr. Munday visited churches and businesses to get their support.

Tank was surprised when twenty-one boys

showed up for tryouts. All of them made the team.

At the very first practice, Tank whispered to Jimbo, "We're so much better than most of the guys on our team. We're sure to be starters."

"Doesn't matter," replied Jimbo. "I'm just glad we finally have a team to play on."

Their first game was against the St. Thomas Catholic School team, the twelfth of July, at three P.M.

All week the Roosters practiced hard. But not hard enough for Tank. He wanted them to hit harder, throw farther, and run faster.

"Come on," he shouted over and over. "We're Roosters. You're playing like a bunch of hens and biddies."

"It's just a game," Jimbo said. "Don't make everything so serious."

"No, it's baseball," Tank insisted. "You play baseball to win." Then to impress his teammates with his skill, Tank held the bat with one hand the way Josh had. Jimbo threw the ball. Tank could tell Jimbo hoped he'd miss. But he didn't. The ball flew far into left field.

Jimbo rolled his eyes.

On Friday, Mr. Munday named the starters. Jimbo was pitcher, Tank catcher—just like Josh Gibson.

Right before they left, Munday passed out white T-shirts with a Red Rooster sewn on the front and red caps. "I wish I had real uniforms for you," said Mr. Munday.

"They look great to us," said a few of the players.

"Hey, I hear Josh Gibson stayed at your house," a boy named Kenny Underhill said, catching up with Tank.

"Sure did," Tank put in. "And he gave us some good advice about hitting."

"Well, I hope you listened good," said Kenny. "We're gonna be playing St. Thomas. I hear they're fierce."

Chapter 12

Show-Off

O n Saturday, in the huddle right before the Roosters took the field, Mr. Munday reminded everybody that they were a team. "There's no place on a team for me-thinking. We are us-thinkers. Now go for it!"

It was a close game until the sixth inning. Then the Roosters seemed to fall apart.

"Don't lose heart," shouted Mr. Munday, clapping his hands. Apollo was beside him with his buckets of water. But no amount of coaxing and no amount of water seemed to help the players.

St. Thomas was at bat, ahead by one run. Willie Johnson, the Red Roosters' center fielder, dropped an easy fly ball, and St. Thomas scored another run. The Roosters were behind 5–3. In the seventh, another error cost the Roosters two more runs.

Jimbo came to bat at the top of the eighth, with two outs and runners on first and second. He fired off a fast-moving grounder to center field, bringing in two runs. Jimbo was on second with the score 7–5. The Roosters had a chance.

The next Rooster batter got on base with a single. Munday told Jimbo to stop at third base and not risk running home. Rooster players were on first and third. Tank stepped up to the plate. He could bring in the tying run. And if he hit a homer, the Roosters would pull ahead! Suddenly Tank dropped his left hand; he held the bat with one hand.

Jimbo saw it and yelled to him. "No, no, don't do it, Tank! No!"

"Tank!" Mr. Munday hollered. "Put your other hand on that bat or else . . ."

Tank didn't listen. This was going to be his moment of glory. He waited for the pitch. He swung and connected with the ball. But it didn't go very far. The catcher scooped up the ball and threw him out with an easy toss to first base.

The rest of the game was a blur. Three quick outs in the ninth, and the game was over. The Roosters lost. Mr. Munday was furious. "You're off the team, Tank."

Tank tossed his cap on the ground and stomped off. "We don't need to be on this losing team. Come on, Jimbo," he said.

"Not this time," said Jimbo. "We had a chance to win, but you threw it away by showing off.

You're selfish and spoiled. And I'm sick of picking up after you. No more!"

Tank threw his arms in the air. "I thought you said it wasn't about winning. It was about having fun. Well, I was having fun. But I'm done with this team!"

"Good riddance," said one of the players.

"You can't play baseball by yourself. You were me-thinking out there, trying that silly move," said Mr. Munday.

"That's what Josh Gibson does, and he's not silly."

"You're no Josh Gibson," said Kenny.

"Josh has experience and power. Besides, he would never risk a game," Munday added. "He does one-handed batting only when the Grays are way ahead."

Tank dropped his head. He knew he was

wrong, because his stomach was flip-flopping the way it had when he'd chewed tobacco.

Jimbo and the others walked away, leaving him alone.

Then someone put a hand on his shoulder. It was Apollo. "I love being a water boy."

Tank smiled. "Hey, Apollo! You did an amazing job today. A much better one than I did."

Chapter 13

Got It!

A few days later, Josh Gibson and the Grays pulled into Nashville for a weeklong three-game series with the All-Stars.

After a meal of fresh corn and fried catfish, Josh joined Tank in the backyard for a game of catch.

Tank told him about the Red Roosters. "But I'm off the team, because I was—"

"Showing off," Josh said. "Jimbo told me."

"Yeah, I lost our first game." Tank swallowed hard. He wanted to cry but didn't. "Jimbo is

still mad at me. So is everybody else. Thank goodness Daddy was at work and didn't see me mess up."

"Hey, li'l buddy, you made an error, for sure," Josh said, sitting down in the grass. "But one player can't lose a game by himself. And no one player can win a game all by himself, either."

"I get it," Tank said softly. "Like Mr. Munday says, I have to stop me-thinking and start us-thinking."

"I call that good-thinking," said Josh. "Now, let's go get you back on the team and in good graces with your brother."

Tank smiled for the first time in days.

Jimbo was on the front porch. The world didn't feel right when Jimbo was mad at him.

"I'm sorry, really sorry," Tank told his brother. "Will you forgive me for being selfish and reckless and—"

"Sure! You're forgiven, but I know sooner or later you'll do something like that again," he said. "That's who you are."

"We're friends again?" Tank asked.

"We're friends and brothers. That's how you get away with the stuff you do," said Jimbo. He tried to keep a serious face, but it didn't hold long. Before long, the boys were laughing and playing catch with Josh. It was almost like nothing had happened. They were like that.

Mr. Munday relented and put Tank back on the team. But Tank had to sit on the bench for two games and suffer the frowns of his teammates.

There was another game with St. Thomas the next afternoon just before the main game. This time Tank was determined to play his best and not show off.

A letter from Lilly Belle arrived in the afternoon mail. She wrote Tank and Jimbo a poem:

Baseball
Fans
In the summer sun
Cheering
Brothers
When the game is done.
Running
Bases
One, two, three.
Playing our best
Whole-heartedly.

With love,
Big Sis

The next day Tank had his sister's poem in his back pocket as he took his place behind home plate.

Josh sat with the Turners. Even Mama came along, though she thought a shortstop held the door open. Several of the Grays were also in the stands.

It was a tough game. The Roosters worked hard.

"Come on, boys," shouted Mr. Munday. He seemed to be having the time of his life, running up and down the sidelines firing off orders and giving encouragement. "We can take 'em!" he shouted.

The second-string catcher hurt his thumb in the seventh inning. Mr. Munday decided to put in Tank.

Now, at the top of the ninth, the score was Roosters 0, St. Thomas 4. With two outs, the Roosters had a runner on second.

Tank was at bat. He stared at the pitcher, trying not to think about anything except the pitch.

A strike came across the plate. The second pitch was a ball. He let that one go. The next three were balls, too. So he walked to first base.

Runners were at first and second when Jimbo came to bat.

"Take your time. Be careful, Jimbo," yelled Mr. Munday.

Tank watched as his brother closed his eyes, wiped his brow, and set his hat. The St. Thomas pitcher studied Jimbo closely. The catcher flashed a signal to the mound. The pitcher shook it off.

"Hang in there," Tank yelled.

The St. Thomas pitcher threw a curveball, except when it got to the plate it hung there, just waiting to be smacked. So Jimbo hit the ball hard and cleared the bases.

There was so much jumping and cheering going on in the Roosters' bull pen you would have thought they'd won the game. In fact, even with Jimbo's home run, the Roosters still lost, 4-3.

"You all played well," said Mr. Munday. "I'm proud."

Mama invited everybody back to the house for lemonade and pound cake. Daddy couldn't stop talking about how Tank and Jimbo had played.

Josh gave the brothers a big thumbs-up. But Apollo said it best. "They won, but we played good."

For the first time, Tank understood how it was possible to lose and still feel good.

Then Josh reached inside his carpetbag and brought out a box wrapped in decorative paper. "My neighbor fancied it up for me," he said. "I told her it was for two special friends of mine— fellow baseball players and all. So, this is for y'all," he said, giving the box to Tank and Jimbo.

The boys tore into it. Inside was a baseball.

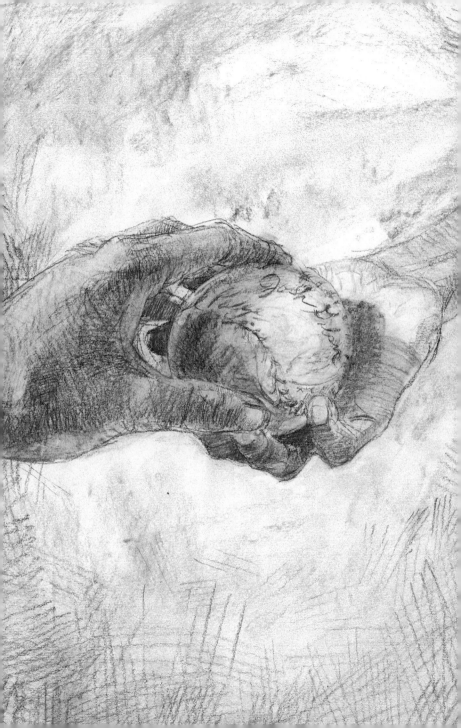

Tank held it in his open palm. Jimbo turned it and read off the signatures. All their heroes on the Grays—and Satchel Paige's autograph, too.

"How'd you get Satchel's?" Tank wanted to know.

Josh just smiled.

"These are the greatest of the greats," said Jimbo.

"We will treasure this forever," said Tank.

Another Scrap of Time

"The Homestead Grays came back to Nashville several more times during the summer of 1937, the year they won the Negro National League Championship." Gee was looking at the team photograph and smiling. "Each time they came to town, Josh Gibson stayed with the Turners. And throughout the rest of his sixteen-year career, Josh remained Tank's favorite player."

"That was a great story," Aggie said.

"Look, I found this old shirt. It has a red rooster on it," said Mattie Rae.

Gee shook her head. "Just a simple T-shirt with a red rooster on it. Remember they grew up during the Depression. There wasn't a lot of money."

Trey was reading an old newspaper article. "It's about Jackie Robinson."

Nodding at Trey, Gee said, "He was the first black player on a major-league team. He played for the Brooklyn Dodgers."

"Who else made it to the majors back then?" Trey asked.

"Satchel Paige finally did. But he was past his greatest days by then."

"What about Josh Gibson?" Trey wanted to know.

Gee looked sad. "No, he didn't, great as he was. He died too soon. But he did make it into the Baseball Hall of Fame. There are twenty-nine players from the Negro Leagues in the Hall of Fame."

"That's a good thing, right?" said Mattie Rae.

She was the youngest, and Trey could see she was losing interest in baseball. She was looking over stuff in one of Gee's shoe boxes.

"Ooh, look. An old report card. The name on it is Violet Turner. Who was she, Gee?"

"One of my cousins. She was the first in our family to go to school with white children. That was in the nineteen fifties, after the Supreme Court decision."

"Tell us about her," asked Mattie Rae. "She got good grades!"

"Next time," said Gee. "I promise."

About This Story

J osh Gibson and Buck Leonard were both stars for the Homestead Grays, one the most famous teams in the Negro Leagues. At the time my story takes place, in the late 1930s, the Grays' home base was just outside Pittsburgh, Pennsylvania. The Tennessee All-Stars and their ballpark, however, are fictional. Like many other cities, Nashville had no Negro League team, but Negro League teams like the Grays often did play against a local team like my made-up All-Stars. These "Exhibition Games" did not count toward league standings, but fans got to see some of the great players in action. The practice was called "barnstorming."

Because most hotels, especially in the South, did not allow blacks to stay in them, Negro League players often stayed in private homes during away games. It must have been an incredible experience for kids like Tank and Jimbo to have a real-life sports hero sleeping in the next room!

The days of all-black baseball came to an end in the early 1950s once major-league teams began hiring black players. Jackie Robinson was the first. Satchel Paige played one season for the Cleveland Indians. But most of the Negro League greats were past their prime by this time.

Patricia C. McKissack

Timeline

Some Highlights of Negro Leagues Baseball

+ **1800s:** Blacks play on integrated teams in the early days of pro baseball. But by the turn of the twentieth century, baseball changes to reflect the social structure of the country, which is segregated.

+ **1920:** By the 1920s black players are locked out of major-league baseball. So Rube Foster organizes the Negro National League, the first black baseball league to last more than a year. The Negro Southern League is also formed.

✦ **1930:** On July 25, 1930, eighteen-year-old Josh Gibson catches in his first Negro League game for the Homestead Grays. Gibson had been in the stands, but when the Grays catcher hurt his hand, the manager asked Gibson to step in. Josh Gibson moves to the Pittsburgh Crawfords in 1932, and comes back to the Grays in 1937, just in time to win the Negro National League championship.

✦ **1934:** Buck Leonard, first baseman, joins the Homestead Grays. He plays with the team for seventeen seasons.

✦ **1937:** The Negro American League is started by H. G. Hall. The Homestead Grays adopt Griffith Stadium in Washington, D.C., as their home away from home.

In 1937 the Negro National League teams are:

Homestead Grays
Washington Elite Giants
Newark Eagles
Pittsburgh Crawfords
Philadelphia Stars
New York Black Yankees

In 1937 the Negro American League teams are:

Kansas City Monarchs
Cincinnati Tigers
Memphis Red Sox
Birmingham Black Barons
Chicago American Giants
Indianapolis Athletics
St. Louis Stars
Detroit Stars

+ **1939**: Baseball Hall of Fame opens in Cooperstown, New York. No black players are inducted.

+ **1947**: On April 15, 1947, Jackie Robinson puts on a Brooklyn Dodgers uniform and makes history as the first African American in the twentieth century to play on a major-league team. Tragically, Josh Gibson had died just three months earlier.

+ **1948**: The last World Series of the Negro Leagues is played. Satchel Paige is signed by the Cleveland Indians.

+ **1950**: The Homestead Grays play their last season.

+ **1972**: Josh Gibson, along with teammate Buck Leonard, is inducted into the Baseball Hall of Fame. Jackie Robinson had been inducted in 1962 as the first black player.

✦ **2006**: Seventeen Negro League and pre–Negro League legends are elected into the Hall of Fame, bringing the total number of segregation-era players to twenty-nine, plus six managers/executives.

A Rookie reader®

A Bit Is a Bite

Written by Larry Dane Brimner
Illustrated by Erin Eitter Kono

Children's Press
An Imprint of Scholastic Inc.
New York • Toronto • London • Auckland • Sydney
Mexico City • New Delhi • Hong Kong
Danbury, Connecticut

For Carson and Cassidy Brimner.
—L. D. B.

For Caitlyn Akiko.
—E. E. K.

Reading Consultant

Cecilia Minden-Cupp, PhD
Former Director of the Language and Literacy Program
Harvard Graduate School of Education
Cambridge, Massachusetts

Cover design: The Design Lab
Interior design: Herman Adler

Library of Congress Cataloging-in-Publication Data

Brimner, Larry Dane.
  A Bit is a bite / by Larry Dane Brimner; illustrated by Erin Eitter Kono.
     p. cm. — (Rookie reader: silent letters)
  ISBN-13: 978-0-531-17547-7 (lib. bdg.)   978-0-531-17780-8 (pbk.)
  ISBN-10: 0-531-17547-2 (lib. bdg.)   0-531-17780-7 (pbk.)
  1. English language—Vowels—Juvenile literature. I. Kono, Erin
Eitter. II. Title. III. Series.
  PE1157.B75 2007
  428.1'3—dc22   2006024388

SCHOLASTIC, CHILDREN'S PRESS, A ROOKIE READER, and associated logos are trademarks and/or registered trademarks of Scholastic Inc.
3 4 5 6 7 8 9 10 R 17 16 15 14 13

"Dad, please don't be mad!"

"I know I slid down the rail."

"The rail isn't a slide."

"I guess I ate more than a bit of cake."

9

"A bit is a bite. You ate a big slice!"

"I'm sorry I hid your new shoes."

"WHERE did you hide them?"

"I did jump on the bed."

"Beds are for sleeping—
not for jumping."

"And I accidentally broke your favorite plate."

"This plate is in pieces.
Let's get the glue."

"I know I made some mistakes.
But please, Dad, don't be mad!"

"I'll even give you my special kite."

"You did not make me mad.
You don't need to give me your kite."

29

"It's no fun flying a kite alone.
We can take your kite outside
and fly it together!"

Word List (82 words)

(Words in **bold** have the silent e sound.)

a	did	I'm	more	slid
accidentally	don't	in	my	**slide**
alone	down	is	need	**some**
and	**even**	isn't	new	sorry
are	favorite	it	no	special
ate	fly	it's	not	**take**
be	flying	jump	of	than
bed	for	jumping	on	the
beds	fun	**kite**	**outside**	them
big	get	know	pieces	this
bit	give	let's	**plate**	to
bite	**glue**	mad	**please**	together
broke	guess	**made**	rail	we
but	hid	**make**	**shoes**	where
cake	**hide**	me	sleeping	you
can	I	**mistakes**	**slice**	your
Dad	I'll			

About the Author

A teacher for twenty years, Larry Dane Brimner is now a full-time writer who has penned more than 125 books for children, including several in the Rookie Reader series. Among his titles are *Nana's Hog*, *Nana's Fiddle*, and *Firehouse Sal*. He is also the author of the perennial favorites *Merry Christmas, Old Armadillo*, and *The Littlest Wolf*. He lives in Arizona's Old Pueblo.

About the Illustrator

Erin Eitter Kono has illustrated several picture books including *Nellie and the Bandit*, *Star Baby*, *Passover*, and *Hula Lullaby*, which she also wrote. She is the recipient of the Children's Literature Council's award for "Excellence in a Picture Book."

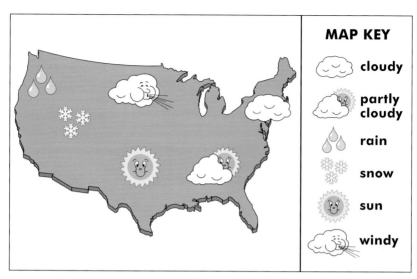

weather map

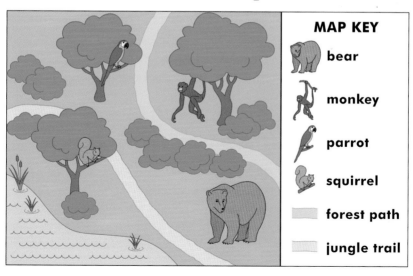

zoo map

31

Index

About the Author

Rebecca Aberg lives in Wisconsin and teaches elementary school. She has written more than 20 books. Rebecca enjoys learning as much as she enjoys teaching others.

Photo Credits

Photographs © 2003: Corbis Images/Richard Hutchings: 3; Leslie Barbour: 5, 30 bottom left; Photo Researchers, NY/Lawrence Migdale: 29.

Maps by XNR Productions